To Rebecca
John —

Two Angels (for Sure)
Thanks for your
beautiful words.
Believe!

Pat Montaldo

OTHER BOOKS BY PAT MONTANDON

Making Friends
(THE FIRST SOVIET-AMERICAN PUBLICATION)

The Intruders

How to Be a Party Girl

C E L E B R I T I E S

A N D   T H E I R   A N G E L S

Celebrities
and Their
Angels

PAT MONTANDON

RENAISSANCE BOOKS
Los Angeles

A portion of the author's royalties will go to the
Children As The Peacemakers foundation

Get involved with the Children As The Peacemakers foundation by contacting:
Celebrityangels@aol.com

Web site:
http://www.audience.com/douglas/peacekids/

Copyright © 1999 by Pat Montandon

10 9 8 7 6 5 4 3 2 1
Design by Lisa-Theresa Lenthall
Published by Renaissance Books. Distributed by St. Martin's Press. Manufactured in the United States of America. First Edition

With immense love this is dedicated to . . .

Sean Patrick Wilsey, my son, whose unfailing kindness and compassion sustains me

Daphne Beal, my daughter-in-law, whose presence enhances my life

Lillian Howell, an earthly angel without artifice and with unparalleled generosity

My parents, Reverend Charles Clay Montandon and Myrtle Taylor Montandon, who taught me to believe

My siblings, Faye Antrim, Glendora Hill, Charles Montandon, Nina Stiverson, and James Taylor Montandon, who always encourage and support my dreams. The late Dr. Carlos Montandon and baby angel Betty Ruth Montandon

Angelic friends Jane Robb, Merla Zellerbach, Leonardo Perillo, Delia Erlich, and Lisa Stephens

The many angelic beings, seen and unseen, who hover around me, protecting me, guiding me, giving me hope.

CONTENTS

A few years ago, I had an extraordinary experience which inspired me to ask celebrities for their sketches of angels. The drawings were used for a Gathering of Angels event that benefited a project to stop the killing of America's youth. And now, with additional sketches and text, we have this delightful book.

Perhaps that's why the image appeared, first to my housekeeper Cecelia, and then to me, so we could spread the word about angels.

On an October evening in 1993, I met with a group of volunteers. We were anguished by the random acts of savagery affecting our nation's progeny, and were creating a half-mile-long banner of white silk to be emblazoned with the names of 8,000 kids slain in California during a ten-year period. The Banner of Hope was to serve as a wake-up call for America. "The angel spirits of the children who have been so brutally wrenched from us, will guide this project," I said, as we closed our meeting.

The next morning as warm raindrops fell, Cecelia was ironing in the guest room, and I was listening to a tape of harp music. Credulity is strained, I know, but I began to have a hankering for angel food cake.

When Cecelia came upstairs for lunch I asked if we had any cake mix.

"I didn't think you liked angel food cake," she responded.

"I don't usually," I laughed. "Goes with the music, I guess."

Afterward she went downstairs to finish the ironing, and I decided to try my hand at cake baking. I had just begun gathering the ingredients when I heard a shout from downstairs.

"Ms. Montandon, you'd better come down here, there's something you need to see." Cecelia's voice carried a note of urgency.

Hurrying down the stairs I came to an abrupt halt as Cecelia, hands shaking, pointed to the center pane of the wide guest-room window. There, in a silvery circle like a daytime moon, was a complex design of, well, I didn't know what.

"It was there this morning, but it went away, so I didn't say anything," Cecelia said. "It looks like a garden of shimmery stuff."

"There's a butterfly too. See the wings?" I was inspecting the apparition closely.

"There's nothing on the other windowpanes except steam from the iron." Cecelia was clearly uneasy. "What could it be?"

The hair on my arms stood up as I got my Polaroid and began taking pictures of the manifestation. I paused only long enough to call my neighbors, Lois Boomer and Althya Youngman.

"Hurry," I said. "There's something you should see and I don't know how long it will last."

Cecelia and I remained transfixed, absorbing the image. What appeared to be an intricate flower garden covered the lower third of the circle. On the left side of the image was a cross, the top of which looked like a looped ribbon, or an infinity sign. In the center of the design a scalloped three-dimensional arrangement formed the base from which a childlike face appeared, and then wings. But I never thought of the word "angel" until my neighbors arrived.

"Why it's a Baby Angel, a Cherub," Lois said.

Cecelia looked shaken. "I've been praying to the angels."

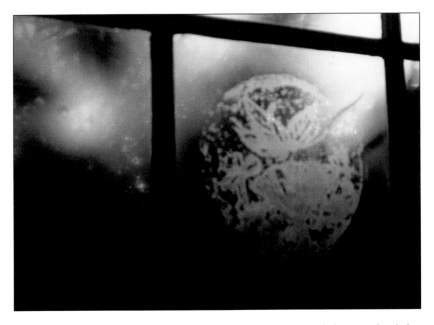

the image on the window

Althya, an eighty-six-year-old woman who at one time lived in India as a follower of Mahatma Gandhi, said, in a matter-of-fact way, "Oh yes it's an angel, all right. I see them around here all the time."

When I inspected the phenomenon from outside the house it was apparent the depiction was within, as the prismatic substance bulged away from the glass. The radiant chimera lasted forty-five minutes before fading away, leaving no evidence on the windowpane of having been there.

Cecilia desperately wanted to make the angel reappear. She duplicated the way she had been ironing, the temperature of the room, and ran steaming water into the bathtub, but her efforts were to no avail.

Afterward, when parents of murdered children came to see me, I told them about the apparition and showed them the pictures. Each one felt the delicate tracery of a winged being was the spirit of their child, and they were comforted.

Children epitomize all that's beautiful, good, and innocent. Marc Klaas understands this better than most. The father of Polly, so cruelly abducted from her home and murdered, writes of his encounter with an angel after his daughter was killed. His story, along with a picture of Polly, graces this book.

On one occasion after my experience, I attended a luncheon on the top floor of a San Francisco skyscraper. I had brought photographs of the image to show to my friends, even though I was aware that I might be ridiculed. After I told them my story, I held up the enlarged images for viewing, but their focus was elsewhere. Puzzled, I turned to follow their gaze. Beyond the plate-glass windows, as if on cue, was a double rainbow.

Skeptics will chide, but I'm certain divine spirits exist. They are here to guide, protect, comfort, and give us hope. If my experience is an indication, they have a delectable and goofy sense of humor.

So, if you hunger for angel food cake and harp music, you could be headed for an encounter with a heavenly messenger.

. . .

CELEBRITIES
AND THEIR ANGELS

Oprah Winfrey
ACTOR & TALK-SHOW HOST

19

Dianne Feinstein
U.S. SENATOR

Don Novello
COMEDIAN & ACTOR

Я хотела бы
чтобы все надежды
и мечты детей
сбывались.   Р. Шищ 16. iv 1993.

I hope that all the hopes and wishes of the children will come true.

Raisa Gorbacheva
FORMER FIRST LADY, U.S.S.R.

Mikhail Gorbachev
FORMER U.S.S.R. PREMIER &
NOBEL PEACE PRIZE WINNER

23

*H*ere is Sam Lamott's painting of an angel. The artist, who is three-and-a-half years old, informs me that it is a long angel, and the blue parts are the sky. God bless you.

Annie Lamott
WRITER & MOTHER

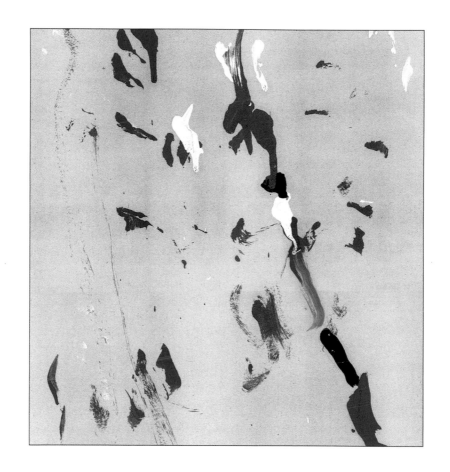

Sam Lamott
ARTIST & SON OF ANNIE LAMOTT

Pour moi les animaux sont des anges – Je vis entourée par les anges à quatre pattes qui embellissent ma vie –

Par contre le démon prend souvent la forme humaine des chasseurs, des fourreurs, des vivisecteurs, des tueurs d'abattoirs –

On tue les anges car on ne sait pas qu'ils sont des anges

Mais moi je le sais et j'essaye de les protéger car ils me protègent.

Brigitte Bardot

27 Août 1998

Brigitte Bardot
ACTOR

*F*or me, animals are angels. I am surrounded by four-legged angels who embellish my life.

On the other hand, the devil often takes the human shape of hunters, fur traders, vivisectors, and slaughterhouse killers.

Angels are killed as one does not know they are angels.

But I know it and I try to protect them because they protect me.

Brigitte Bardot

Oops! There goes another angel right now.

Richard Simmons
FITNESS INSTRUCTOR

Loretta Lynn
SINGER

When I decided to preach a sermon on angels, I found practically nothing in my library. Upon investigation I soon discovered that little had been written on the subject in this century. This seemed a strange and ominous omission. Bookstores and libraries have shelves of books on demons, the occult, and the devil. Why was the devil getting so much more attention from writers than angels? Some people seem to put the devil on a par with God. Actually, Satan is a fallen angel.

Even when people in our modern age have had their attention drawn to the subject of angels from time to time, those ideas have often been fanciful or unbiblical. As I write this a popular television program tells the story of an "angel" who has been sent to earth in the form of a man to help people who are facing problems. . . . [It] reinforces the idea . . . that angels are just a product of our imagination, like Santa Claus or magical elves. But the Bible stresses their reality, and underlines their constant—if unseen—ministry. . . . In a materialistic world which . . . is riddled with evil and suffering, we need to discover afresh the Bible's teaching about angels. . . .

The English painter, Sir Edward Coley Burne-Jones, wrote to Oscar Wilde that "the more materialistic science becomes, the more angels shall I paint: their wings are my protest in favor of the immortality of the soul."

The Bible teaches that angels intervene in the affairs of nations. God often uses them to execute judgment on nations. They guide, comfort, and provide for the people of God in the midst of suffering and persecution. Martin Luther once said, in *Table Talk,* "An angel is a spiritual creature without a body created by God for the service of Christendom and the church."

As an evangelist, I have often felt too far spent to minister from the pulpit to men and women who have filled stadiums to hear a message from the Lord. Yet again and again my weakness has vanished, and my strength has been renewed. I have been filled with God's power not only in my soul, but physically. On many occasions, God has become especially real, and has sent His unseen angelic visitors to touch my body to let me be His messenger for heaven, speaking as a dying man to dying men.

Reverend Billy Graham
EVANGELIST

I believe God has SENT US
angels —they are the children
of the world! *EdAsner*

Ed Asner
ACTOR

Angela Alioto
ACTIVIST

I don't think I have had any experiences with angels but there just may be a guardian, one who sits on my shoulder and keeps me out of serious trouble most of the time. A guardian angel doesn't let you lose your temper very often and, after you lose it, you immediately go back and apologize to the people you have lost it with. It also makes you do the toughest things first in your life instead of doing the pleasant ones first and putting off the others. A guardian angel cheers you up when you are blue, congratulates you and pampers you when things are doing well. Now that I think of it, I'm sure there is a guardian angel someplace close by in my life.

Helen Gurley Brown
EDITOR & AUTHOR

Sasquatch is my angel because he is the only one in his species and he controls the UFOs with his mind control.

Steven Hanft
DIRECTOR

I was named after the angels, since I was born during Christmas. So they have always been an ally for me, and have always appeared in my doodles for years. This specific angel appeared one day as I was working on a huge creative project that was due the weekend of November 19–20, 1988. While on the phone, creatively problem-solving some challenging places in the project, I drew this angel. Somehow, after drawing the angel, the project began to move again.

Angeles Arrien
ANTHROPOLOGIST

Angeles Arrien

$\mathcal{I}$ believe that angels are whatever shape, size, sex, color, disposition, et al you create in your own mind. The only aspect about angels that is definite and universal is their strong dislike for prejudice, bigotry, hatred, ethnocentricity, narrow-mindedness, and broccoli.

David Brenner
COMEDIAN

$\mathcal{I}$n my view, angels work through living persons and there are lots of them in this world. I am sure I have met a few. They are the people who give us a helping hand when we need it, lift us up when we are down, and offer us encouragement when things appear bleak. They ask for no thanks; they are just happy in seeing someone succeed or achieve their contentment.

Hank Hartsfield Jr.
ASTRONAUT

*H*e loves you and me—just believe.

Ronnie Lott
FOOTBALL PLAYER

$\mathcal{E}$ver since I was a little girl I have felt I've had a guardian angel to show me the way.

Marlo Thomas
ACTOR

Adam Siegel
ARTIST & MUSICIAN

ANGELIC MOMENTS

I know they are here and all around us!
Some of them are invisible and

   some of them have four legs and live at home with us!

Always remember to treat everything and everyone with respect

   because you may be entertaining an angel!

Linda Blair
ACTOR

Hal Riney
ADVERTISING EXECUTIVE

MY ANGELS

My angels travel with me everywhere. They are my inner guides that bring me ideas and intuition on "what to do" and "how to do it" in the sweet now and now.

Angels are inspired beings of light and illumination. I am in the business, as a professional motivational speaker. I am blessed that my angels have always and in all ways answered my question, "What can I say to help this person or this group of people?" The response to my talks from the people who attend is, "Thank you. That's just what I needed to hear!"

Mark Victor Hansen
AUTHOR

Burt Reynolds
ACTOR

Barbara Boxer
U.S. SENATOR

When I was little, I figured out that God wouldn't have much time to listen to my prayers, but I heard that He had assistants—lovely invisible ladies called "angels," who flew around the earth helping people.

One of these angels, I knew, was assigned to look after me, I named her Glena (not quite "angel" backwards, but close), and she had almost unlimited magical powers—if she liked you.

. . . One day I was walking home from grammar school when along came two boys. They started teasing me—about my pigtails, the braces on my teeth, everything—and though I wanted desperately not to cry, I was just about to break down. Suddenly, an angelic vision appeared and I heard Glena's voice in my ear! I can't remember her words, but I know she inspired me to growl whatever the seven-year-old's equivalent of "Get lost!" was—and darned if the boys didn't . . . run away.

I've never seen Glena again, but she taught me a good lesson about standing up for my rights. She knows what it's like to be teased . . . because you're different. After all, she's the only brunette angel in Heaven.

Merla Zellerbach
WRITER & EDITOR

Merla Zellerbach

Polly Klaas

*D*uring the course of one year I lost my only child to violence, my youngest brother to the ravages of illness, and a grandmother to time. I survived these tragedies a better, stronger, and more determined person, because I was nurtured by the grace of angels.

The hand of God touched me on the day Polly was born. The first time I held her in my arms I experienced the power of unconditional love. This perfect baby was mine, and I would love and protect her forever. For me, this was the miracle of birth.

I was fortunate that Polly was my companion on this earthly pilgrimage. The strength of her commitment enhanced my understanding of the human condition and provided me with a clarity of vision. The depth of her emotion taught me that caring for others could strengthen my own self-worth and expand my horizons beyond material values. The purity of her love defined her final act. She faced her worst fears with courage worthy of the most seasoned combat veteran. On shaky knees, as the devil was stealing her into the night, her final words were, "Please don't hurt my mother and sister." My greatest teacher was only twelve years old.

That night the angels dipped their wings over Petaluma and re-claimed one of their own. In life Polly shared her gifts with those who were touched by her presence, but in death she touched us all. The welfare of a little lost girl surmounted religious, ethnic, and political barriers. Millions of eyes were looking for her and millions of hands were clasped in prayer for her safe return. Her presence on earth set a course that millions of years of evolution, thousands of years of legislation, and hundreds of years of struggle and strife couldn't accomplish. She brought us together as one. These were Polly's angels.

. . . For sixty-five days we navigated the murky waters of despair toward a fate that tantalized us with glimmers of light, then doused our hopes with uncertain veils of darkness. Finally the prayers of Polly's angels were answered, but not as we expected. Polly's unselfish bravery in the face of doom provided the target, and her commitment of love gave us the weapon to use in the eternal struggle between good and evil. In bitter irony we discovered that in order to win the war, we sometimes have to lose a battle.

Seven months later I visited my brother Jonathan on his deathbed. He seemed to be recovering and was excited to see me. I held his hand as he told me the following story:

"Earlier today Polly visited me. She fluttered above me like a butterfly on tiny wings. I asked her why her wings were so small. She said that it was because she wasn't ready to go yet. Then Polly said, 'Get ready, Uncle Jonny, because you will be joining me soon and there are a great big pair of wings waiting for you.' I asked her if I should hurry. Polly said, 'No, Uncle Jon, you want your wings to get as big as they can, and together we will take a ride that is better than anything at Disneyland.'"

Two days later Jonathan died. Now he is with Polly on a fantastic voyage.

My grandmother was very old, bedridden and fragile, so we didn't tell her about either of these misfortunes. . . . She is now with Polly, the sun has set, and I know something that I never realized before. The angel we were seeking was guiding us all along.

Marc Klaas
ACTIVIST

*A*ngels are everywhere, they are different sizes, shapes, and colors, they don't discriminate. Angels are kind and compassionate, they present themselves on a daily basis, they bring a smile to your face, and they touch your heart. They affect people's lives in a profound way. Angels can be you and me.

I was devastated when Michael died, but I would turn on the television set and there he would be—my angel.

Cindy Landon
WIDOW OF MICHAEL LANDON

$\mathscr{A}$ngels are God's thoughts that comfort me when I'm afraid.

Dyan Cannon
ACTOR

Loni Anderson
ACTOR

May your Angels be
with you
wherever you are —
with Love ♡
Joni James

Joni James
SINGER

I believe in the spirit, and that angels—traditional winged, haloed angels—are a metaphor for the spirit. Wings represent the ability to take flight and transport themselves through time and space, and a halo, divine and infinite light.

The spirit is something we all possess within our human forms (bodies)—these bodies are for transporting our spirit (which is who we are) while we are grounded on earth in the physical.

Our spirits (we) are infinite energy which animates the bodies we are assigned. The body is an essential tool for the spirit because the spirit is energy and cannot be seen; therefore the body is representation of the spirit's existence, and is the tool which allows the spirit to maneuver and to achieve physical tasks while grounded in this physical world until the spirit is released upon physical death. The spirit is infinite; therefore, although the body dies, the spirit goes on.

I believe that if one could actually see angels or the spirit . . . it would be made up of an ethereal energy that circulates infinitely. . . .

Jeffrey Smith
MUSICIAN

Jeffrey Smith

LET THE MAGIC BEGIN

*S*omehow our inner magic collides with our outside reality and we forget the strength of our inner resources. Fear takes over, and our natural ability to create our own solutions gets lost in the mire of the circumstance. But, if we can learn how to stay connected to this natural source of magic, we can fully utilize the abundant, blissful energy of the Universe that is available to us at every moment. We can literally create "heaven" right here on Earth.

The true challenge of life as I see it, is to stay connected to this natural source of energy. . . .

Our personal magic begins when we find our own method of staying connected to this source. And by simply awakening to, understanding, and flowing with this connection, we begin to reach the full depth, richness, and potentiality of our lives.

Cathy Lee Crosby
ACTOR, PRODUCER & AUTHOR

Marsha Mason

$\mathcal{R}$esponding to the question "Do you believe angels exist?"—yes.
Why? Because I've seen and heard them.

Marsha Mason
ACTOR

$\mathcal{A}$ngels are with us each and every day. Each day we need to remember how fortunate we are to be alive and healthy.

Amelia Anka
DAUGHTER OF PAUL ANKA

Olga Korbut
GYMNAST

63

$\mathcal{Y}$ou can not see the angel [on the facing page], but she is there. She doesn't like to have her picture drawn because people will stop her on the street. But she's there. I know because I saw her once.

Art Buchwald
HUMORIST

bless
the moon-blessed
★ night-mind ★
big-mind ★
- Buddha-mind -

deathless   heart

Peter Coyote
ACTOR

THE DALAI LAMA

*N*ow we are nearing the end of the twentieth century . . . people in the scientific disciplines are taking a fresh interest in spiritual and moral concepts and are prepared to reappraise their attitudes towards the relevance of spiritual development in order to achieve a more complete view of life and the world. . . . I am optimistic that over the next few decades there will be a great change in our worldview both from the material and the spiritual perspectives.

Tenzin Gyatso
HIS HOLINESS THE DALAI LAMA

learning to fly...
yours,
Joan Baez

Joan Baez
SINGER

Chuck Negron
SINGER

*A*ngels come in different forms. Some fly, some soar, and some nuzzle. My angel is a dog, a real nuzzler named Daisy.

When my wife, Eileen McGann, and I returned from the Democratic National Convention in Chicago in August of 1996, our lives were in ruins. Every newspaper in the nation screamed the news that I had resigned as President Clinton's campaign strategist due to a sex scandal. Mobs of reporters crowded the driveway to our Connecticut home, shouting questions, blocking our car, and banging on the windows as we attempted to pass.

Life, marriage, and career all seemed over.

The next day, one of our very dear friends arrived, cuddling a seven-week-old golden retriever puppy in her arms. The . . . tiny dog had no idea that she was coming into the middle of a firestorm. . . .

She didn't know that I was in disgrace, a reprobate, an object of scorn and ridicule. She had no notion that our marriage was in tatters and that we faced a bleak future.

But she did know that she wanted to be cuddled, held, stroked, petted, fondled, tickled, rubbed, and kissed. . . . She burrowed her wet little nose under our hands to push them into proper petting position. . . .

. . . We caught her contagious love, her curiosity, her joy of living. She helped bridge the gulf between us. . . .

Demanding, imperious, persistent, relentless, she would not settle for anything less than our total, undivided love and attention. She brought warmth into our lives at a time that God knew we needed it. She came to symbolize the need to continue, to move on, to love again.

There are no coincidences. She arrived at our darkest hour, sent by the Lord. She is our angel. Instead of wings, she has big floppy ears. Instead of a halo, she has wide black eyes with deep pools of empathy. Instead of a wand, she has a long nose with a wet, black tip. But she is an angel of God, sent to help us live and remember how to love. She is the angel of life.

Dick Morris
POLITICAL ANALYST

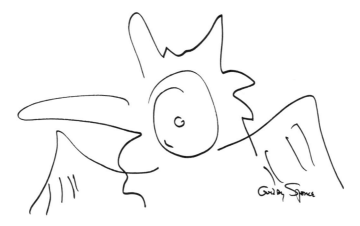

*A*ngels have one eye. They see all and fly.

Gerry Spence
MOTIVATIONAL SPEAKER

Dean Edell
PHYSICIAN

ANGELS

A wonderful story in the Orthodox tradition tells us that before every person go two angels calling, *Make way, make way for the image of God!* We need that constant reminder—we are all of us made in God's image and are therefore infinitely precious. We have not only been created by God, but also bought at an incredible price—a marvel that the angels themselves wish they could understand.

Every mention of angels in the Bible seeks to remind us that God is interested in us, cares about us, loves us enough to get involved in the goings-on on this little planet. They stand before God on our behalf and serve us on behalf of God.

Angels, like parables and fine poetry, speak in many layers of meaning and mystery, trying to express the inexpressible. If we ignore them, our lives are the poorer.

When you see your morning face in the mirror, try greeting your guardian angel, too. When you encounter your friend, a neighbor, or a stranger, offer his or her angel a silent acknowledgment, and heed their message that the person you are facing is made in the image of God.

Crazy as it may sound, this little habit of acknowledgment can give us a sense of the greater reality when all that we see and feel is but a shadow.

Bishop Desmond Tutu
ANGLICAN ARCHBISHOP OF CAPE TOWN

$\mathcal{I}$ am my own angel, for the gods need a lot of help and they—the gods—help those who help themselves.

Eartha Kitt
SINGER

Christina Grof
AUTHOR

Whoopi Goldberg
ACTOR

Whilst touring in a play with my sister Juliet I was thrown from a horse—the saddle slipped as I was attempting to mount and the horse flew into a panic, reared up, bucked, and twisted in the air. I flew up and off and landed heavily upon my back, missing a jagged rock by millimeters. I was badly winded, shaken, and in pain, but otherwise all right. It was a lucky escape and I felt strongly that I'd been protected, that my angel had been there—all that day I felt that protection. Just before I left these friends' house I found a small card on the mantelpiece which read, "There's an angel on your shoulder."

Hayley Mills
ACTOR

As I looked into the eyes of this great spirit,
time suspended, and my soul bowed in
reverence at the vast creation that she is
for what she's seen and what she knows,
like an angel, she opens her heart to me, opening
mine, healing with love and acceptance.
I am lost in her, in the way of being found
to care for her
to learn from her
to be humbled by her
to set her free that she may rightly roam the
secret corners of this Earth
keeping the balance
striving for harmony
and protecting us all in ways that only she can. . . .

Sheryl Lee
ACTOR

Bill Griffith
CARTOONIST

The "angelic moments"? I experienced a countless number of those: When I hear some beautifully played Mozart, Schubert, or when I am in the presence of Rafael's or Boticelli's work or read some Pushkin or Keats or just walk though the Finnish forests and lakes with my wife.

Vladimir Ashkenazy
PIANIST & CONDUCTOR

Chang Shu Wu
ARTIST

MY ANGELS

*M*y angels are within and without

They fly on the wings of my trust

When I love without fear

They dance on the wind

And make snow angels in the dust

When a child totters on the brink

I send her my love, not my fear

She may fall with a thump

Or land on her feet

My angels take care of the dear

My angels are what I observe

They are energy, there all the time

If I ignore it or doubt it

Or make up some gods

Then I have forgotten what has always been mine

We are life at its best and its worst

We don't need to look away or above

We are the universe singing

We are all that there is

We are angels in need of our love

Holly Near
SINGER & COMPOSER

$\mathcal{H}$erbert Gold's guardian angel has no definite shape because he or she has to be ready to move in any direction, depending on the trouble heading his way. It could be love, it could be a meter maid, it could be sushi left out in the sun.

(Portrait of guardian angel drawn from memory. Without lifting pen from paper except to indicate a loving and caring eye.)

Herbert Gold
WRITER

Shari Belafonte
MODEL & ACTOR

ONE LOVE

Father Miles Riley
PRIEST & COMPOSER

*R*eal love is more than popularity

You can't count in quantity

Not measured like stuff

Kathie Lee Gifford
TELEVISION HOST

*T*his statue is the best depiction of my guardian angel, "Frederique," that I've ever found. Dozens of my workshop audience members have reported seeing Frederique standing behind me, and they all give the same description: she's roughly six feet ten inches tall, she looks just like me, and she's a translucent opal-white color. Frederique has helped me in so many situations. She is my constant companion, guide, and source of comfort. I thank God that we all have guardian angels to watch over us.

Doreen Virtue
WRITER & LECTURER

*S*ometimes a man, in serving God, can only do as angels do, and wing it.

Garry B. Trudeau
CARTOONIST

I believe everyone has their own image of angels, so the readers should fill in how *they* think of angels.

Angels are the souls of good. They reign as supreme messengers in all people.

God Bless!

Janet Leigh
ACTOR

Lin Evola
ARTIST

Not like Dante

    discovering a commedia

           upon the slopes of heaven

I would paint a different kind

      of Paradiso

in which the people would be naked

      as they always are

         in scenes like that

      because it is supposed to be

        a painting of their souls

but there would be no anxious angels telling them

    how heaven is

      the perfect picture of

a monarchy

and there would be no fires burning
    in the hellish holes below
    in which I might have stepped
nor any altars in the sky except

fountains of imagination

Lawrence Ferlinghetti
POET

Connie Mack
U.S. SENATOR

Marilyn Horne
OPERA SINGER

"A house is not a home
unless it has an Angel!"

June Lockhart
ACTOR

. . . *Y*ou arrived cautious and curious. You had been

　　shopping for smells, and you bought a bubble-

gum smelling eraser, a root beer lip gloss brush, a bottle brush,

　　a bottle of cologne.

—Do you play chess? you said in the second minute.

At the Empire State, when we hit the big view at the

　　Top—you took it in your own time. You were Loch Lomond.

You like: typewriters, jigsaw puzzles, chocolate,

　　pianos, grape soda, three in a phone booth, Pez,

　　playgrounds and limousines. And most of all, it

　　seemed, was playgrounds—the carriage ride we took

　　to the carousel (where you rode the inside horse)

　　charmed your daddy and me . . .

So my goodbye kiss is to the beautiful wake you leave

　　behind your beautiful course Kathryn.

　　the tribute of the current to the source

Art Garfunkel
SINGER & COMPOSER

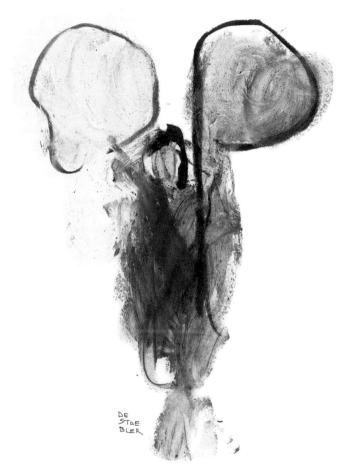

Stephen de Staebler

SCULPTOR

*S*ometimes, when I close my eyes and think of Nicole, I get a smile on my face because she is an angel—she is our angel.

Juditha Brown
MOTHER OF NICOLE BROWN SIMPSON

Robert Mondavi
VINTNER

*T*he word "angel" is a difficult word to measure people with. I have my "angels" but they are in what is called "heaven." In other words, my angels come from God and come with God. I have very strong spiritual commitments. I am a Yogi and a devotee of the oldest yogi lineage in the world—Siddha Yoga. My Guru, the head of the Siddha Yoga lineage, is an angel sent from God to help people through their trials. Her spiritual name is Gurumayi Chidvilasananda. She is a Great Being, as was Moses, Buddha, Mohammed, Jesus Christ, etc.—all great saints . . . Great Beings. To sit at her feet as I have done in what is called Darshan, which means, in Sanskrit, kneeling to be blessed . . . placing your head below your heart . . . is, I feel, quite the same as it must have been two thousand years ago to kneel before Jesus Christ. Gurumayi and her Swamis (monks) are my angels. I pray to Gurumayi as I pray to God to help me through my problems, to bless those I love, to bless the food I consume, and to forgive my sins. This my real angel and to be able to do what I do is why I consider her my angel.

Richard Adler
COMPOSER

Virgil Burnett
ARTIST & WRITER

Making angels in the snow

Everyone can be an angel —
Cindy Crawford

Cindy Crawford
MODEL

$\mathcal{N}$o church has ever spoken authoritatively on what angels look like. If they are truly spiritual creatures, as many of us have been taught, then it logically follows that they don't look like anything since they cannot be seen.

In my view the important contribution that the world's thousands of separate religions can make is in inducing their adherents to live lives that are ethically and morally admirable. I have never been favorably impressed by those who behave in the most depraved, acquisitive, selfish, and sometimes even sinful way but, on the other hand, profess to believe in the literal existence of angels.

If there is a God, as I assume, then one of his greatest gifts to humankind—one not granted to the other millions of animal species—is that of reason.

Steve Allen
PERFORMER & WRITER

Show me an angel and I'll paint one.

Gustave Courbet
ARTIST

Gerald McDermott

ARTIST

Ellen Kreidman
AUTHOR

*M*erlin was as black as the night in which I found her, weighing less than a pound, in Golden Gate Park. Neither one of us should have been out so late, especially a baby like Merlin, and especially in the park. Scooping her up I carried her home under my sweatshirt next to my heart.

A few months after Merlin came to live with me I had cervical spine surgery. When I came home from the hospital, wearing a hard plastic collar, struggling to do the most ordinary things, that little cat seemed to understand. She became my constant companion. At night she would wait, perched on the top of my headboard until I finally settled in, and then with a meow, would jump down, curl up next to me with her head on the pillow her paws across my neck, and purr.

Merlin and the cypress tree were intimately acquainted, as she once climbed to a top branch and then sat there howling, until rescued. The glorious tree guarded the entrance to the Enchanted Cottage, and was at least a hundred years old. Along with a twin, it sheltered my home from passersby, provided shade and beauty for the entire neighborhood, and became a cherished member of my family.

During the horrific wind and rains of 1997, in a resounding earthquake of sound, one of the two trees was blown over, wrecking four cars, injuring a woman, and undermining my sleep. From that moment on, whenever the wind blew, I would gaze at the survivor, praying its roots would hold fast, that it wouldn't fall. When I had it checked by an arborist, he said the cypress was near the end of its life, that I should have it cut down. But I couldn't bring myself to part with my friend. And then I read about a tree just like mine falling and killing a man, which sent me into a tearful leave-taking.

The angels must have been listening because the next day a tall, gaunt man, his long hair in a ponytail, rang my doorbell. He introduced himself as Jack Mealy.

"I'm a sculptor," he said. "And I would love, really love, to carve something from that tree."

"Can you carve an angel?"

"Sure can." Opening his portfolio he showed me samples of his work. One sculpture revealed an exquisite violin being born from a piece of driftwood. Half of the musical instrument emerged in shel-lacked splendor from the grayness of the mother.

"Finding the angel within is what I do."

Scaffolding soon ringed the cypress stump and I feared the irritating noise of a chain saw would create fissures in the usually quiet neighborhood. Would my neighbors tolerate such noise for six months? The length of time the artist would need to create the angelic being.

But they seemed not to mind, and, like folks fascinated by a construction site, became enthralled by what we were doing. Every day people stood around talking to Jack, slowing the work, dawdling. Merlin was equally enamored and would sit at the base of the tree for hours watching the progress of an angel being born as if she understood the significance.

"Why are you taking the bark off?" a sidewalk superintendent asked. "I like the bark."

"Oh, that's just the outer skin." Jack was covered with sawdust. "Just like people. The outside doesn't always match what's inside. You've gotta find it."

the sculpture in process

We were enthralled to see Jack release a soaring wing from within the tree.

"There really is a heavenly spirit in that tree." A woman was watching with keen interest. "I'm going to take a picture for my altar."

Fascinated by the effect our endeavor had on others, I thought of the essential spirit that lives inside us. The angel we can set free by connecting with those who are near but seem distant because of the moat we dig around ourselves, our property, our tree, our angel, claiming ownership of that which no one can own.

As the sculpture neared completion, flowers and votive candles were often left on the root base—and, in response to the message on a plaque, donations for Oprah's Angel Network. There was an enigmatic message of hope flowing from the angelic carving, a communication I welcomed as I was recovering from a brutal divorce, and the death of Merlin, my beautiful pet. She is buried under a covering of baby tears and in the shadow of angel wings.

The site has not only become a tourist attraction but also a spiritual touchstone.

One morning, outside, in the luster of a pink sunrise, I could see the large angel sculpture—her wings were spread, her hair flowing in a river of wooden tendrils, eyes turned heavenward. And then I heard the flutter of wings, real wings. A silver-gray morning dove had been resting on the arm of the angel, and as I watched, the bird stretched its feathers wide, raised its head, tucked its feet under its belly, and lifted off from the cherubic runway, flying slowly toward me. The silver-white creature circled twice in front of my window, unhurried, mystic.

"What are you doing here?" I said aloud to the dove. "You don't belong in this neck of town."

From two feet away his bright eyes seemed to be communicating with me. Another lazy circle and he landed on the limb of an olive tree. After pecking at it he expanded his glossy wings once again, flapped twice and with a soft *coo* flew off to meet the rising sun.

"Go in peace," I whispered as I watched the feathered messenger, buoyed by rays of light, disappear into the limitless void.

. . .

CONTRIBUTORS

RICHARD ADLER
Songwriter and composer who collaborated with Jerry Ross on the musicals *The Pajama Game* (1954) and *Damn Yankees* (1955); now a writer of concert music and television commercials.

ANGELA ALIOTO
Former president of the San Francisco Board of Supervisors. She is an attorney and national children's activist.

STEVE ALLEN
Actor, host, musician of stage and television, songwriter, and author of many books.

LONI ANDERSON
Played Jennifer Marlowe on television's *WKRP in Cincinnati* (CBS, 1978–82). She can be seen most recently in the film *A Night at the Roxbury* (1998).

AMELIA ANKA
Daughter of Paul Anka—singer, composer, and one of the biggest teen idols of the late fifties; he wrote "My Way" for Sinatra and "She's a Lady" for Tom Jones.

ANGELES ARRIEN
Anthropologist and author of *The Four-Fold Way: Walking the Paths of the Warrior, Teacher, Healer, and Visionary; The Tarot Handbook: Practical Applications of Ancient Visual Symbols;* and *Signs of Life: The Five Universal Shapes and How to Use Them.*

VLADIMIR ASHKENAZY
Conductor and musical director of the Royal London Philharmonic Orchestra from 1987 to 1995. He is also one of the world's finest pianists, having won many major international competitions.

ED ASNER
Star of *The Mary Tyler Moore Show* for which he won five Golden Globes and seven Emmys. He was inducted into the Television Academy Hall of Fame in 1996. He can be seen most recently in *Hard Rain* (1998).

JOAN BAEZ
Singer and activist. In addition to her well-known musical career, she is the founder of the Institute for the Study of Nonviolence and is the author of several books.

BRIGITTE BARDOT
Actor. Her American debut, *And God Created Woman* (1957), created a sensation. In 1985 she was decorated with the Légion d'Honneur in France.

SHARI BELAFONTE
Model, actress, and daughter of Harry Belafonte. She has appeared on over 300 magazine covers.

LINDA BLAIR
Actress celebrated for her unforgettable role in *The Exorcist* (1973), for which she won a Golden Globe. Her last film role was 1996's *Prey of the Jaguar.*

SENATOR BARBARA BOXER
Senator (D) California. Former journalist and editor of *Pacific Sun.*

DAVID BRENNER
Perennial talk-show guest who was recently appointed honorary president of the Children's Rights Council.

HELEN GURLEY BROWN
Former editor of *Cosmopolitan* magazine. *World Almanac* named her one of the twenty-five most influential women in the United States.

JUDITHA BROWN
Mother of Nicole Brown Simpson.

ART BUCHWALD
Pulitzer Prize–winning columnist whose work is syndicated in over 550 newspapers.

VIRGIL BURNETT
Artist, illustrator, and writer. He lives in Canada.

DYAN CANNON
Academy Award–nominated actress for *Bob and Carol and Ted and Alice* (1969). She has recently appeared in *Out to Sea* (1997), and *Ally McBeal* (Fox Television, 1997–).

CHANG SHU WU
Famed Chinese artist from Beijing.

GUSTAVE COURBET
French painter (1819–77) who cofounded the Realist movement.

PETER COYOTE
An accomplished actor who has appeared in more than sixty films, most recently *Patch Adams* (1998) and *Random Hearts* (1998). He has also narrated over fifty documentaries and fourteen audiobooks.

CINDY CRAWFORD
Supermodel and actress who has appeared on over 600 magazine covers.

CATHY LEE CROSBY
She is the original Wonder Woman and author of the motivational book *Let the Magic Begin: Opening the Door to a Whole New World of Possibility*. She can be seen most recently in TV's *A Memory in My Heart* (1999).

STEPHEN DE STAEBLER
Winner of fellowships from the National Endowment for the Arts and the Guggenheim Foundation for his sculpture, which is currently displayed in museums around the country.

DEAN EDELL
Nationally syndicated television and radio advice doctor. Twenty million fans tune in weekly to hear what the Cornell Medical School graduate has to say.

LIN EVOLA
Fine artist, teacher, and writer.

SENATOR DIANNE FEINSTEIN
Senator (D) California. Former mayor of San Francisco and recipient of numerous prestigious awards. She has worked to improve U.S.-China relations.

LAWRENCE FERLINGHETTI
Beat poet and founder of San Francisco's City Lights Books, the country's first all-paperbound bookstore.

ART GARFUNKEL
One-half of the multiple Grammy Award–winning duo Simon and Garfunkel, and 1990 Rock and Roll Hall of Fame inductee. He is also the author of a book of poetry titled *Still Water.*

KATHY LEE GIFFORD
Cohost of the long-running *Live with Regis and Kathy Lee* television show.

HERBERT GOLD
Writer of over twenty books. He has received fellowships from the Guggenheim, Ford, and Rockefeller Foundations. He has won the Sherwood Anderson prize for fiction.

WHOOPI GOLDBERG
Oscar-winning stage and screen actor and regular on television's new *Hollywood Squares* (1998–). She can be seen most recently in the films *Girl, Interrupted* (1999) and *How Stella Got Her Groove Back* (1998).

MIKHAIL GORBACHEV
Former Soviet premier and winner of the 1990 Nobel Peace Prize.

RAISA MAXIMOVA GORBACHEVA
Women's advocate (1932–99) and former first lady of the U.S.S.R.

REVEREND BILLY GRAHAM
Evangelist, presidential advisor, and prolific writer and author.

BILL GRIFFITH
The cartoonist of *Zippy the Pinhead*. His comics are syndicated in over 200 newspapers.

CHRISTINA GROF
Founder of the Spiritual Emergence Network, cocreator of Holotropic Breathwork, founder of Grof Transpersonal Training, Inc., and author of several books.

TENZIN GYATSO, THE DALAI LAMA
The fourteenth Dalai Lama. He has governed Tibet while exiled in India since the Chinese takeover in 1959.

STEVEN HANFT
Director of music videos for the Cure, Beck, Hootie and the Blowfish, and Mercury Rev.

MARK VICTOR HANSEN
Contributor to the bestselling *Chicken Soup* book series.

HANK (HENRY WARREN) HARTSFIELD JR.
Crew member of *Apollo 16* and *Skylab* missions *2, 3,* and *4*. He received several medals of merit from NASA and won the *National Geographic* White Space Trophy in 1973.

MARILYN HORNE
Renowned mezzo-soprano opera star and winner of four Grammy Awards. She debuted in 1954 as Hata in *The Bartered Bride* at the Los Angeles Guild Opera.

JONI JAMES
She first gained recognition in the 1950s, and became the "Queen of the Albums" during her nearly two decades as "Her M-G-eMinence" at MGM Records.

EARTHA KITT
Singer. Took over the role of Catwoman on TV's *Batman* (1966–68) after Julie Newmar left the series. Eartha got her start as a dancer. She appeared with Eddie Murphy in 1992's *Boomerang*.

MARC KLAAS
The father of Polly Klaas, the young girl from Petaluma, California, who was abducted and murdered. Founder of the Klaas Foundation for Children.

OLGA KORBUT
Olympic gold medalist in 1972 for the Floor Exercise and the Balance Beam. She won the team gold that year and at the 1976 Olympics in Montreal.

ELLEN KREIDMAN
Relationship expert and bestselling author of *The 10-Second Kiss*.

ANNIE LAMOTT
Teacher and author of *Traveling Mercies, Bird by Bird,* and *Operating Instructions*.

SAM LAMOTT
Son of bestselling author Annie Lamott, Sam was the subject of her book *Operating Instructions*.

CINDY LANDON
Widow of Michael Landon, star of *Little House on the Prairie* (NBC, 1974–82) and *Highway to Heaven* (NBC, 1984–89).

SHERYL LEE
Actor who played Laura Palmer in David Lynch's *Twin Peaks* (ABC, 1990). She won the Women in Film "Spirit of Sundance Woman of the Year" award in 1995.

JANET LEIGH
Actress and mother of Jamie Lee Curtis. Her defining role was as Marion Crane in *Psycho* (1960). She acted alongside her daughter in *Halloween H2O: Twenty Years Later* (1998).

JUNE LOCKHART
She recently appeared in the film remake of the *Lost in Space* television series (CBS, 1965–68) in which she once starred. She also played Ruth Martin on television's *Lassie* for six years.

RONNIE LOTT
A former safety for the San Francisco 49ers and holder of four Super Bowl rings. He played in ten Pro Bowls.

LORETTA LYNN
Country-western singer and the "Coal Miner's Daughter." She was the first woman to receive the Country Music Association's "Entertainer of the Year" award.

GERALD MCDERMOTT
A Caldecott Medal–winning author and illustrator best known for his children's books which explore Native American and African cultures.

SENATOR CONNIE (CORNELIUS) MACK
Senator (R) Florida. Son of baseball great Connie Mack. He is chairman of the Republican Conference, the Joint Economic Committee, and the Economic Policy Subcommittee for the Committee on Banking, Housing and Urban Affairs.

JOE MARTIN
Syndicated cartoonist.

MARSHA MASON
Two-time Golden Globe winner for the films *Cinderella Liberty* (1974) and *The Goodbye Girl* (1977). She has also been nominated for four Oscars. She can be seen in *Nick of Time* (1995).

HAYLEY MILLS
Daughter of Sir John Mills and novelist Mary Hayley Bell. As a young girl in the early 1960s she appeared in such movies as *The Parent Trap* (1961) and *That Darn Cat!* (1965). As an adult she starred in *Good Morning Miss Bliss*.

ROBERT MONDAVI
Vintner and cocreator of the Napa Valley Wine Auction, the proceeds of which are donated to several San Francisco Bay Area hospitals.

DICK MORRIS
Political consultant, author of several books, including *Vote.com*, political commentator for Fox News, and former advisor to President Clinton and Senator Trent Lott.

HOLLY NEAR
Singer. *Ms.* magazine's 1985 Woman of the Year. Her one-woman show *Fire in the Storm* has taken her all over the country.

CHUCK NEGRON
Lead singer of the rock band Three Dog Night that hit number one with the singles "Joy to the World," "Black and White," and "Mama Told Me (Not to Come)."

DON NOVELLO
Creator of the character Father Guido Sarducci on *Saturday Night Live*. Novello has appeared as Father Sarducci in movies—*Casper* (1995)—and on Fox Television's *Married . . . With Children* (1987–97).

BURT REYNOLDS
Star of such films as *Deliverance* (1972) and *Smokey and the Bandit* (1977). Recently seen in *Striptease* (1996), *Boogie Nights* (1997), and *Mystery, Alaska* (1999).

FATHER MILES RILEY
Winner of three Emmys and ten National Gabriel Awards (among others) for his ministerial work in film, television, stage, and radio.

HAL (PATRICK) RINEY
Advertising executive and winner of seventeen Clio Awards, fifteen Addy Awards, the Grand Prix du Cannes, and five Lion d'Or du Cannes Awards.

ADAM SIEGEL
Graffitti artist and musician who has played with bands such as the Infectious Grooves, the Eels, Excel, and My Head.

RICHARD SIMMONS
America's favorite diet-and-fitness expert, author, and star of over a dozen exercise and cooking videos.

JEFFREY SMITH
Jazz vocalist whose latest album is titled *Down Here Below.* He starred in the Paris production of *Cabaret* and has sung for Claude Bolling's big band.

GERRY SPENCE
Celebrity defense lawyer and bestselling author of books such as *Give Me Liberty!: Freeing Ourselves in the Twenty-first Century.*

MARLO THOMAS
Actress best known for her starring role in television's *That Girl* (ABC, 1966–71), and the special *Free To Be . . . You and Me* (1974). Daughter of Danny Thomas.

GARRY B. TRUDEAU
Syndicated cartoonist. Creator of *Doonesbury,* a comic strip that satirizes national politics and social trends.

BISHOP DESMOND TUTU
Archbishop of Cape Town, South Africa. 1984 Nobel Peace Prize winner.

DOREEN VIRTUE
Author of several books including *Divine Guidance* and *Divine Perscriptions,* and an expert on angels.

OPRAH WINFREY
Talk-show hostess for which she has won five Emmy Awards. As an actress she most recently starred in *Beloved* (1998), Jonathan Demme's film of the Toni Morrison novel.

MERLA ZELLERBACH
Former columnist for the *San Francisco Chronicle,* author of ten books, and editor of the *Nob Hill Gazette.*

Pat Montandon and her "children"

ABOUT THE AUTHOR

Pat Montandon, the seventh child of Texas ministers, has written four books, was a columnist for the *San Francisco Examiner*, hosted a television talk show, and lectures extensively. In 1982 she created Children As The Peacemakers, a nonprofit foundation that allows children to voice their concerns about nuclear war to dozens of world leaders.

In 1983 Pat launched the International Children's Peace Prize. In 1986 she created the Banner of Hope, a mile-long red silk memorial inscribed with names and ages of children killed in war. Seven years later she created the California Banner, a half-mile of white silk imprinted with names of eight thousand children murdered in California. In 1987 she brought the first Soviet child on a peace mission to the United States, and initiated international Peace Kids Peace Clubs. She took supplies to famine victims in Ethiopia and Armenia. In 1992 she distributed seventy tons of food to Russian kids. She was honored with the United Nations Peace Messenger Award and nominated for the Nobel Peace Prize. Her fifth book is *Whispers from God*.